D0452179

BROCCOLI
FOR THE BRAIN

BROCCOLI
FOR THE BRAIN

75 Puzzles and Exercises
to Boost Your Brain Power!

MICHEL NOIR, PH.D.

Mc
Graw
Hill

New York Chicago San Francisco Lisbon London Madrid Mexico City
Milan New Delhi San Juan Seoul Singapore Sydney Toronto

Copyright © 2008 by Scientific Brain Training (SBT). All rights reserved. Printed in China. Except as permitted under the United States Copyright Act of 1976, no part of this publication may be reproduced or distributed in any form or by any means, or stored in a database or retrieval system, without the prior written permission of the publisher.

1 2 3 4 5 6 7 8 9 10 11 12 13 14 15 16 17 18 19 20   SDB/SDB   0 9 8 7

ISBN 978-0-07-150820-9
MHID   0-07-150820-1
Library of Congress PCN 2007930317

Scientific writing
Sandrine Bélier, Ph.D.
Bernard Croisile, Ph.D.

Exercise design
Sandrine Bélier, Stéphanie Bouvet, Bernard Croisile, Michel Noir

Text
Stéphanie Bouvet

McGraw-Hill books are available at special quantity discounts to use as premiums and sales promotions, or for use in corporate training programs. For more information, please write to the Director of Special Sales, Professional Publishing, McGraw-Hill, Two Penn Plaza, New York, NY 10121-2298. Or contact your local bookstore.

This book is printed on acid-free paper.

Contents

Preface

Have you ever found it difficult to remain focused during a long speech or presentation or to solve a problem when there was too much going on around you?

We've all been there. No one is able to stay perfectly focused for any long period of time—it's physically impossible. However, while there might be nothing that can keep us from falling asleep in the middle of a boring opera, it is possible to improve our attention capabilities and ability to focus—and this book will show you how.

Like any other mental skill—such as remembering or doing math in your head—you can increase your ability to focus and to pay attention if you work on those skills. That is precisely what you will find in this book: more than fifteen different types of exercises and games scientifically designed to improve your attention and focusing skills.

To fully benefit from these exercises, it is recommended that you find a nice, quiet place to do them—no children, pets, or loud spouses allowed!—and give them your full attention. Whatever you do, don't try to rush through these exercises or to do them all in one sitting! As you do the exercises, if you feel your focus start to drift significantly, stop and do something else and come back to them later. Trying to forge ahead when your mind is tired doesn't do your brain cells any good.

Ready? Set? Concentrate!

Introduction

What Is Attention?

We've all been through times when we haven't been able to focus on the task at hand or have found ourselves drifting off and daydreaming while something else was going on. But why does this happen? What are "attention" and "focus" exactly, and how do they work? How can we improve them?

Attention and Focus

The terms attention and focus are often used interchangeably—but do they refer to the same thing? Surprisingly, the answer is no. Although attention and focus are interdependent and complementary to one another, the mechanics of each process are significantly different. Let's take a look.

Attention relies on the sensory receptors in our brain that process hearing, sight, smell, touch, and taste. Attention corresponds to the way the mind processes an external event (a sound, image, smell) or an internal event (a thought or feeling) and then sustains this event at a certain level of awareness. For example, when you see someone on a stage and hear them singing a song that reminds you of your childhood, you pay attention.

Focus, on the other hand, is a process that requires a higher degree of this kind of awareness. Its role is to make an abstraction of nonrelevant data—to block out the unnecessary background noise of the people sitting next to you unwrapping a piece of candy or of the heads of the people in front of you, for example—and therefore drastically reduce the scope of the field of attention necessary for a given situation. Focusing is a willful act, one that maintains attention at its highest level.

These processes are interdependent: the more focused you are on something, the less aware you are of what is going on around you; and if you are very aware of everything that is going on around you, you will find it very difficult to focus on something in particular.

The Various Components of Attention

Attention is a complex cognitive function and is a major area of interest in neuropsychology and cognitive psychology, and with good reason—it is absolutely necessary to the correct cognitive functioning of people. As we will see now, there are several components to the phenomenon of attention.

Selective or Focused Attention

At virtually every moment of our lives, our sensory receptors are being stimulated. It is impossible to process all of this information in detail at any given moment. Therefore, these different bits of information and the effect they have on our sensory receptors are in a bit of competition with one another for our attention. Our selective attention selects the bits of information that should be processed first according to their relevance to the situation at hand or what we need in a particular context. Selective attention enables us to focus on something while mentally ignoring all the nonrelevant information without having to physically separate from it. It is therefore absolutely necessary to action and to the way our mind works.

A good level of selective attention implies knowing how to discriminate good information from bad and how to resist interference from unnecessary bits of information. In some people suffering from a high distraction level, attention is easily caught by irrelevant items—something as simple as a stray noise or an unexpected smell can completely throw them off course. Therefore, to be focused and truly pay attention, they have to reduce the number of environmental stimuli that could distract them from being focused—for instance, they may have to find a quiet place to be able to really listen to something carefully.

Selective attention can be strengthened with exercises—for example, exercises in which you have to pinpoint which one element of a group of things is not like the other things.

Shared or Divided Attention

The capacity to divide our attention among several activities at once is known as shared or divided attention, and it is crucial to the simultaneous attention to several tasks. This is the kind of attention that allows us to walk and chew gum at the same time. It requires a logical distribution of our attention resources according to the requirements of each activity.

A routine situation in which we have to perform two tasks at the same time, such as having a conversation while driving home, requires very few attention capacities. It is the same for things in which we have a high level of expertise—there are many expert piano players who can carry on a conversation while they play without even being aware that they are doing it! On the contrary, when we are faced with unusual situations (or activities for which we have a low level of expertise), such as driving in a place we have never been before and trying to find our way to a given location while talking to a passenger, the allocation of attention resources will be more difficult to plan and implement. In the same way, the higher the number of items we have to focus on, the more we will need attention resources, as we'll discover if we are ever driving in a place we've never been before while talking to a friend while trying to play piano at the same time!

Sustained Attention and Vigilance
Sustained attention kicks in when we have to maintain a certain level of attention over a long period of time and in a continuous manner. This kind of attention is necessary to engage in activities with a regular and abundant flow of information, such as driving or playing a sport like basketball, for instance, which require paying constant attention to all the things that are changing and moving.

It is different from vigilance, however, in that vigilance is simply maintaining a level of awareness over a long period of time so that we'll be able to respond quickly to events when they actually do occur. The perfect example is fishing: we can wait for hours on end, but then we will need to react quickly and adequately when the fish (finally!) bites.

Attention Alerts
Attention is strongly dependent on the external factors in our environment—what's going on around us at any given time—but also on internal factors—things like our mood, motivation, priorities, energy levels, how interested we are in what's happening, etc. Attention alerts help us to manage these factors.

- **The Tonic Alert.** Also called wakefulness, the tonic alert is especially sharp during the first part of our day. This wakefulness needs to be combined with sustained attention to enable us to carry out physical activities that may last a bit.

- **The Phasic Alert.** This is a sudden and temporary change in the level of our attention because of an external event—somebody bounds into a room when we're trying to meditate, or another car comes out of nowhere and hits us, for example. This kind of event will completely disengage us from the activity at hand for a certain amount of time, according to the importance of the event we're trying to focus on.

Attention Disorders

Some aspects of attention may be altered by factors such as fatigue, stress, alcohol, and drugs. Below is a list of the main attention disorders and their causes.

Aging

Aging frequently impairs the speed of information-processing capacities, which then reduces the capacity for selective attention. Researchers have shown that the capacity to resist unimportant stimuli and to keep paying attention to the task at hand is particularly faulty in aged people, who are therefore much less efficient when two tasks have to be carried out simultaneously. So, while a twenty-year-old might not experience any difficulty studying while music is playing in the background, a sixty-year-old will find it quite tricky.

Hyperactivity

People with hyperactivity or attention-deficit disorders often have very inflexible attention. Hyperactive people will find it extremely difficult to focus on something and will constantly get distracted by both internal and external events. These people are too aware of irrelevant information and outside stimuli and, as a result, have a hard time focusing.

It is necessary to teach these individuals (most often children) to develop their attention and focus capacities at an early age. Recent Canadian studies, for example, have shown how important regular cognitive training sessions can be in treating these attention-deficit disorders.

Cranial Trauma

Attention disorders are frequently encountered after a cranial trauma. These disorders often manifest themselves by a reduction in the speed of information processing. Studies specifically show that shared attention often suffers after such a trauma, whereas focused attention capacities usually remain intact. One rehabilitation method for improving damaged shared attention consists in having the patient carry out two tasks at the same time. At the beginning, these tasks are very simple (clapping hands while saying the alphabet), then they get more and more complex (driving on a simulator while having a conversation).

Orienting Attention: Automatic or Controlled Process?

If you've been paying attention to the different definitions of attention described above, you'll notice that attention can be both automatic and controlled. It is automatic (i.e., extremely quick and basically out of your control) when attention is guided by an external stimulation, such as when you turn your head in the direction of a loud noise. This is exogenous attention.

In other cases, orienting your attention can be controlled, or made willingly, such as when you choose to pay attention to the ball during a game of tennis. This is a much slower process than exogenous attention, is partly accessible to awareness, and takes up more of your energy. This is called endogenous attention.

For example, exogenous attention is called into play when your attention is drawn to sudden lightning in the sky. But if you control your attention by looking at the sky for stars, that it is endogenous attention.

Scientists get their kicks by trying to control attention processes that are usually automatic. There's a famous test called STROOP that tries to do just that. It consists of having subjects try to read aloud "blue," "yellow," "orange" even though the color of the printed word may or may not correspond to the actual meaning of the word. For example, read the following words aloud:

Blue	**Green**
Yellow	**Blue**
Purple	White
Orange	**Red**

How did you do? The aim of the exercise is precisely to train you to control your automatic attention process and force your endogenous attention to seize control.

The Role of Attention

Attention is the brain process that enables you to learn. Think of it: in order to learn anything, you have to pay enough attention to what experts or teachers have to say or have enough attention to read a book so that the information and new knowledge can be memorized. Without attention, there would be no new material to memorize or master!

Improving and Increasing Your Attention Capacities

It's clear that all these different kinds of attention are essential to our daily lives and happiness, and, as a result, each one requires rigorous training. That's what this book is for, and thanks to the varied exercises and difficulty levels, you'll soon be able to boost your attention and focusing abilities!

Easy
Exercises

Pencils Up!

Link the eight red round figures on this page without raising your pencil.

You cannot touch the other circles or the squares, and you cannot go between two figures more than once!

What's the point?

This exercise trains your capacities for visual discrimination by forcing you to focus on only the red round figures while mentally blocking out everything else on the page.

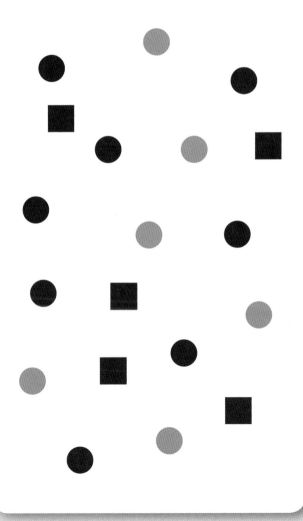

Pencils Up!

Link the eight blue triangles on this page without raising your pencil.

You cannot touch the other triangles or the squares, and you cannot go between two figures more than once!

What's the point?

This exercise is slightly more difficult because your attention has to focus on both color (blue) and shape (triangle).

Pay Attention to Words

You have one minute to memorize the six words below, without looking at the second half of the page.

SOFT	**HAPPINESS**
RUDE	**DEER**
TURTLE	**GREEDY**

Now hide the words above and answer these three questions:

1. How many adjectives were there?
   What were they?

   _____

2. How many animal names were there?
   What were they?

   _____

3. Were there any abstract concepts?
   If so, what were they?

   _____

Tips

Come up with some mnemonics to memorize the words more easily.

Group the words by categories or focus on their first letters.

Pay Attention to Words

You have one minute to memorize the six words below, without looking at the second half of the page.

FRIEND	**ALPHABET**
CARAMEL	**FRIGHT**
PINE	**FOLLY**

Now hide the words and answer these three questions:

1. How many words started with the letter "F"? What were they?

   _____

2. How many trees were listed? What were they?

   _____

3. What was the longest word on the list?

   _____

What's the point?

This exercise calls upon your short-term memory, also called working memory. Short-term memory can store information for about one minute. Its storage capacity is limited because it can store only about seven different items simultaneously.

It Takes Two

Which two geishas are exactly alike?

Tips

The two identical geishas have one very small detail in common. Once you find this distinctive detail, you'll be able to make a match!

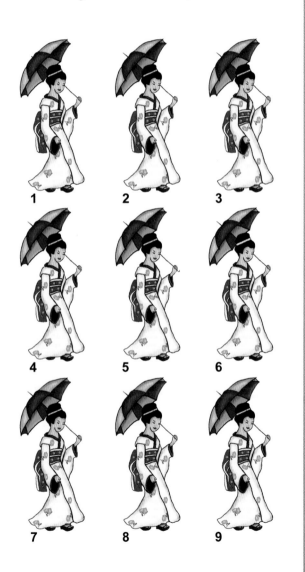

1 2 3

4 5 6

7 8 9

It Takes Two

Which two birds are exactly alike?

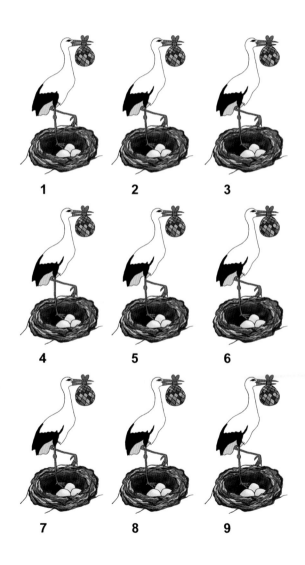

What's the point?

While this exercise requires concentration, it also works your capacity for visual attention and analysis.

The Right Words

Read the text below, paying particular attention to the adjectives.

The legend of the Loch Ness monster has its roots in 565 A.D. According to a historical report, St. Columbus managed to make the dangerous monster hide in the depths of the Loch after it tried to attack a man. With the help of local superstitions, the legend of the Loch Ness monster grew over the centuries until 1933, when the monster became a true tourist attraction thanks to a press article that claimed it was alive and well. People came from all over the world to try and spot it, and the strangest tales about the monster were told to whoever wanted to hear them. Scientists spent long hours exploring the lake for a trace of the monster, but the mystery remains.

Hide the text. Which adjectives below were used in the story?

strangest	**funniest**
dangerous	**intact**
real	**short**
true	**local**
popular	**long**

Tips

In this exercise, you might be tempted to focus only on adjectives and blank out the rest of the text. However, reading the text as a whole will help you put the adjectives into context and remember them more easily.

The Right Words

Read the text below, paying particular attention to the adjectives.

> Compared with modern towns, the size of medieval towns was ridiculously small. As a point of comparison, maybe twenty thousand people lived in the whole of London during its earliest years. This does not mean that towns were unimportant; the political importance of London in times of crisis was very great. Because of this, cities and towns soon began to flourish. By the end of the thirteenth century, there were nearly two hundred small cities and boroughs in England, each with its own distinct history. Unfortunately, fires were frequent at the time, and many of these small cities were sometimes almost totally destroyed.

Hide the text. Which adjectives below were used in the story?

distinct	**frequent**
medieval	**historical**
gorgeous	**new**
great	**approximate**
usual	**modern**

What's the point?

The last two exercises call upon your verbal short-term memory.

Easy as One-Two-Three

Take a careful look at the figure below and count the number of squares it has.

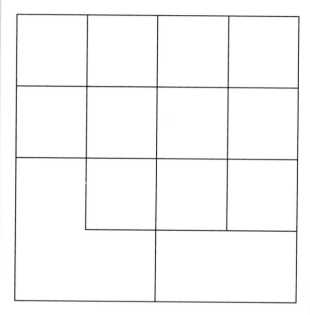

What's the point?

This exercise trains your visual attention and spatial relations.

Focusing on the points where the lines intersect might help you isolate the right number of squares.

Easy as One-Two-Three

Take a careful look at the figure below and count the number of squares it has.

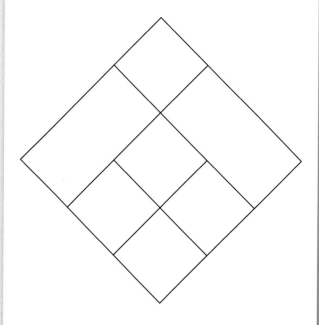

Tips

It might help to determine how many different sizes of squares there are in the figure. Once you've done this, it might be easier to count them.

Sounds Like . . .

Read the text below and write down all of the "sh" sounds.

She was so well-liked and respected in the neighborhood that no one suspected that she had been cheating on her husband for years! She aroused absolutely no suspicions. She went to church week after week and confessed the most hideous sins to the parish priest without any sense of shame or remorse. Her friends were quite sure she was honest and good natured and had no idea how depraved she really was!

What's the point?

This exercise primarily strengthens phonetic recognition and focused attention.

Sounds Like . . .

Read the text below and write down all of the "f" sounds.

> As Philip drank his coffee, he silently prayed for things to go smoothly. Tracking Sarah down in the jungles of the Philippines was just the first phase of the plan. Getting her on the plane and bringing her home was going to be the tricky part— Philip would be foolish to think otherwise. If Sarah didn't feel safe back in Akron, she would certainly flee once again. For this plan to work out to the satisfaction of everyone involved, he would have to be exceedingly careful.

What's the point?

This exercise tests your ability to focus on phonetics, the scientific study of the sounds of human language.

People who suffer from phonetic dyslexia have an imprecise perception of words. As a result, they tend to mix up sounds when they are close phonetically—"B," "V," and "P" sounds, for example.

The Missing Tile

Which of the three tiles below completes the picture?

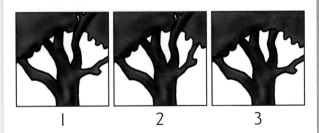

1	2	3

What's the point?

This exercise works your visual attention and ability to process mental imagery. Mental imagery enables you to move each tile in your mind and place it in the figure. This same process allows you to imagine shapes, sounds, smells, and sensations.

The Missing Tile

Which of the three tiles below completes the picture?

Tips

Checking the colors of a tile's borders is a good place to start to see if it will fit into the figure.

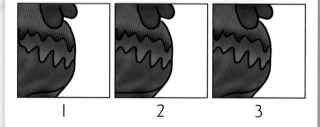

1   2   3

Word Search!

Find the ten words hidden in the grid. They can be read horizontally, vertically, or diagonally; backward or forward; up or down. The same letter can be used in several words.

HINT: the theme is **music**.

What's the point?

This exercise requires visual attention, visual and spatial exploration, and also thematic analysis, as there is a common theme to all the words.

```
Z  E  D  E  N  K  D  K  Y  S  K  B
C  B  C  V  S  L  Z  G  P  M  E  S
T  E  B  S  Y  L  T  P  M  E  E  D
E  A  L  C  Z  N  U  M  Z  L  R  F
R  B  Z  L  S  Y  M  P  H  O  N  Y
P  S  V  I  O  L  I  N  N  D  D  F
R  D  F  Z  N  G  B  H  B  Y  N  T
E  S  F  B  A  N  D  B  G  P  N  Z
T  R  H  Y  T  H  M  N  U  S  A  A
N  B  J  H  A  T  W  L  O  O  L  Z
I  D  D  F  R  T  S  D  V  C  P  N
W  X  S  S  A  R  G  E  U  L  B  X
```

Word Search!

Find the ten words hidden in the grid. They can be read horizontally, vertically, or diagonally; backward or forward; up or down. The same letter can be used in several words.

HINT: the theme is **food**.

```
G  H  F  Y  G  B  U  I  L  V  N  Z
G  S  F  Q  H  K  S  A  D  F  E  Y
C  V  E  K  N  R  F  X  D  R  B  K
A  V  V  L  E  F  A  D  B  G  C  N
D  A  E  R  B  O  N  I  O  N  Z  S
H  A  G  V  B  A  U  C  X  W  B  S
Q  T  G  B  Z  J  T  S  N  L  M  Y
C  S  I  Z  S  H  O  E  J  I  K  C
D  A  I  S  N  H  M  Z  G  M  R  H
X  P  F  G  H  M  A  I  Z  E  C  B
Z  V  H  Y  J  K  T  D  B  E  V  S
Z  B  A  D  L  I  O  D  F  B  E  Z
```

What's the point?

Similar word search games often tell you exactly what words to look for. Here, your concentration skills are flexed even more because you are only given the general theme.

Alphabetical Disorder

Take a careful look at these two sets of characters. Take one minute to find out which characters appear in the series on the right but not the series on the left.

What's the point?

Comparing series of characters from foreign alphabets stimulates your concentration abilities. The time limit imposed also trains your rapidity and accuracy.

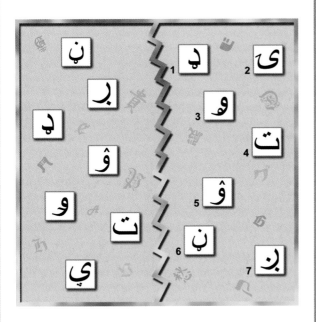

Alphabetical Disorder

Take a careful look at these two sets of characters. Take one minute to find out which characters appear in the series on the right but not the series on the left.

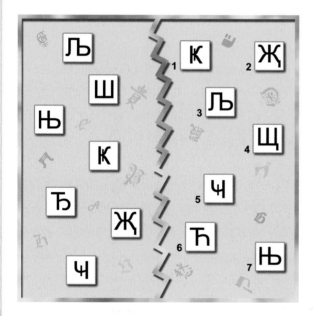

What's the point?

This exercise also improves your attention's flexibility since you have to alternate between the two sets of characters to spot the differences.

What's Wrong with this Picture?

Read the following story and pick out the three things that don't quite make sense.

Ms. Cole was driving. She had just dropped her son Rupert in front of his school and was now driving toward her shop. Her car was absolutely packed with cardboard boxes, all the way up to the roof of her car, from the passenger seat all the way to the trunk. Inside the boxes were dozens of artificial plants that one customer had ordered the week before for a wedding. Suddenly, someone honked a horn at her, and she jumped so high that she literally bumped into the roof of her car. She glanced into her rearview mirror and saw two drivers arguing about a parking space. She would have thought traffic was going to be quieter on Christmas Day.

What's the point?

This exercise calls upon a high number of cognitive abilities. In addition to sharpening your focused attention, reading comprehension and logic also come into play. Mental imagery also plays an important role in this exercise—without it, you wouldn't be able to pick out the bizarre elements.

What's Wrong with this Picture?

Read the following story and pick out the three things that don't quite make sense.

Caroline had been hired in August in the archives department of the public library. She constantly got lost in the five floors of this huge building, patiently strolling along the corridors with her trolley full of books. After one month, the curator permanently assigned her to the fourth floor, which was a great relief to Caroline—she often got lost going from one floor to the other. She was also excited because this top floor of the library contained only the rarest and oldest printed books; some of them were more than seven centuries old! Sometimes she would take a break from work to see her friend in the new books department. She met this friend the very day she was hired, when the two of them had lunch together in a cozy restaurant and passed the time talking about the books they loved while watching the snow fall outside the window.

What's the point?

Reading is a highly complex activity that involves several different brain functions:

- Visual analysis enables you to recognize letters and words.
- Syntax analysis enables you to determine if the sentence structure is correct.
- Phonologic analysis enables you to recognize words when read aloud.
- Semantic analysis brings the meaning into all this and enables you to understand what you read.

The Odd One Out

Find the odd one out in each series.

HINT: the odd one is: ✳

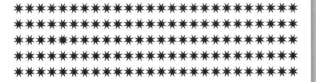

HINT: the odd one is: **✗✗**

HINT: the odd one is: φ

φ φ φ φ φ φ φ φ φ φ φ φ φ φ φ φ φ φ φ φ φ φ φ
φ φ φ φ φ φ φ φ φ φ φ φ φ φ φ φ φ φ φ φ φ φ φ
φ φ φ φ φ φ φ φ φ φ φ φ φ φ φ φ φ φ φ φ φ φ φ
φ φ φ φ φ φ φ φ φ φ φ φ φ φ φ φ φ φ φ φ φ φ φ
φ φ φ φ φ φ φ φ φ φ φ φ φ φ φ φ φ φ φ φ φ φ φ

What's the point?

This is a classic test in cognitive psychology.
It requires:

- attention
- visual focus
- visual and spatial exploration capacities
- shape recognition

The Odd One Out

Find the odd one out in each series.

HINT: the odd one out is: O

HINT: the odd one is: ح

HINT: the odd one is: ❣

What's the point?

Comparison exercises like these not only improve your concentration levels, but can also help you sharpen your comparison skills—figuring out the difference in two pieces of cake or in a $50 skirt as opposed to a $150 skirt—in daily life.

The Connecting Thread

Try to find the logical order of the pictures below.

1

2

3

4

5

6

What's the point?

As simple as it might look, this exercise trains a number of cognitive capacities:

- attention and visual analysis
- planning and strategy-making
- logical reasoning
- mental imagery

Seeing Is Believing

Study the picture carefully for two minutes. Then turn the page for the next step of the exercise.

What's the point?

This exercise trains your visual memory and attention. The level of interaction between memory and attention is high. Attention is particularly called upon when you have to process new information and have nothing to compare it to in memory.

Seeing Is Believing

Answer the following questions:

1. What does the vendor hold in his left hand?

   _____

2. What is the number of the horse leading the race?

   _____

3. Does the woman with a purple suit have a hat?

   _____

4. How many horses are there in the race?

   _____

Seeing Is Believing

Study the picture carefully for two minutes. Then turn the page for the next step of the exercise.

Tips

You have only two minutes to memorize the picture. Here is a small recap of what you should focus on:

- the shape of objects
- their color
- their location in the picture
- their number
- their distance and location to other objects
- details they may contain

Seeing Is Believing

Answer the following questions:

1. What is the color of the vase on the bookshelf?

   _____

2. Describe the painting on the wall.

   _____

3. Is the window open or closed?

   _____

4. Are there books near the television?

   _____

Medium Exercises

Pencils Up!

Link the ten red diamonds on this page without raising your pencil.

You cannot touch the other shapes, and you cannot go between two figures more than once!

Take it to the next level

Now try to link all of the other shapes on the page without touching the diamonds or going between two shapes more than once! You can try this variation on all the levels of this exercise.

Pencils Up!

Link the ten green stars with eight points on this page without raising your pencil.

You cannot touch the other shapes, and you cannot go between two figures more than once!

Tips

This exercise requires visual attention. To succeed, take a careful look at the figures and then mentally trace the track that links them. Then try it with the pencil.

Pay Attention to Words

You have one minute to memorize the eight words below, without looking at the second half of the page.

TEA	**BED**
SOFA	**RENDEZVOUS**
DOCUMENT	**STOOL**
ORCHID	**ROUGHLY**

Now hide the words above and answer these four questions:

1. What was the adverb on the list?

   _____

2. What were the two shortest words of the list?

   _____

3. How many pieces of furniture were listed? What were they?

   _____

4. Were any flower names listed? If so, what were they?

   _____

What's the point?

Apart from visual attention, concentration, and working memory, this exercise also trains your semantic memory—the memory of actual words. This memory contains all the vocabulary you've learned through the years through reading and listening.

Pay Attention to Words

You have one minute to memorize the eight words below, without looking at the second half of the page.

BOOK	**CHILDREN**
NET	**MEDICINE**
BITE	**PIANO**
CRANBERRY	**FERRY**

Now hide the words above and answer these four questions:

1. How many words ended with "erry"? What are they?

   _____

2. What was the plural word?

   _____

3. How many five-letter words were listed? What are they?

   _____

4. What word was associated with fish?

   _____

Tips

If you have problems memorizing these words, saying them aloud might help. Auditory memory is sometimes stronger than visual memory.

It Takes Two

Which two dragons are exactly alike?

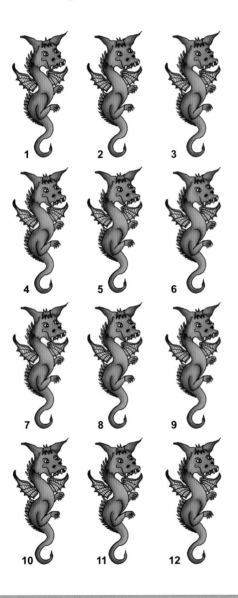

What's the point?

In addition to sharpening your visual analysis and attention skills, this exercise calls working memory into play, because it is necessary to keep your memory active while searching for the two identical dragons.

It Takes Two

Which two policemen are exactly alike?

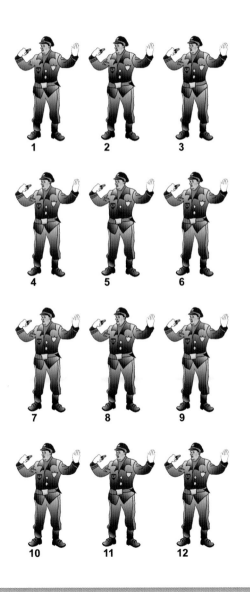

Tips

Rather than considering the images as a whole, it might help to focus on the details of a particular part (head, chest, arm of the character) and then methodically compare the policemen based on those parts. The more details the image has, the more useful is this method.

The Right Words

Read the text below, paying particular attention to verbs.

When Luke realized his cousin wasn't going to show up, he started to feel really sorry for himself. He had traveled a very long way to get to London, and now he was stuck with very little money and no place to stay. He hopped on the tube, went to his friend Johanna's flat, and persuaded her to put him up for the night. Convinced that his cousin had abandoned him entirely, he began to make new plans for his stay in England. Once he did, he found that his mood improved considerably. He and Johanna decided to take a trip up north to Scotland, so one morning they packed their bags and bought their train tickets. They traveled light but experienced some misfortunes and bad encounters until they reached the destination.

Tips

Underline words that you find of particular interest. Reading the story aloud or writing it down somewhere might help improve your concentration levels. Whatever method suits you, remember: do not rush. You can only succeed at this exercise by being really focused on it.

Hide the text. Which verbs below were used in the story?

realized	**packed**	**smiled**
found	**plunged**	**showed**
traveled	**went**	**convinced**
discovered	**made**	**abandoned**
unraveled	**persuaded**	**experienced**

The Right Words

Read the text below, paying particular attention to verbs.

The Queen enjoyed a rare moment of peace as she watched her daughter Gloriana play hide and seek on the terrace with her friends among the old stone vases and the statues covered with moss. How beautiful the princess was, thought the Queen. How young and fresh she looked among the old stone vases and the ancient statues covered with moss. It was hard to believe that her little girl was only ten years old and that one day she would rule the entire kingdom. The Queen stood up and walked over to the window to better appreciate the view from the palace window and briefly entertained the notion of joining her daughter in her childish games. She thought better of it, however, and summoned her maid to help her prepare for the ball.

Hide the text. Which verbs below were used in the story?

grew	enjoyed	stood up
play	walked	glared
cooked	sit up	watched
entertained	run	listened
shook	appreciate	stared

Take it to the next level

If your attention and focus capacities are really good, you can make this exercise even more difficult by doing something in between memorizing the story and answering the questions. For instance, you might say the alphabet aloud twice. Or count to one hundred by fives.

Easy as One-Two-Three

Take a careful look at the figure below and count the number of triangles it has.

What's the point?
The recognition of shapes is an aspect of attention and memory that is frequently used in daily life.

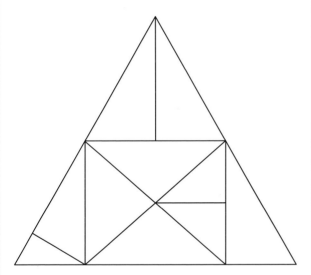

Easy as One-Two-Three

Take a careful look at the figure below and count the number of triangles it has.

Take it to the next level

To work your brain even further, figure out the number of isosceles triangles, equilateral triangles, and right-angle triangles.

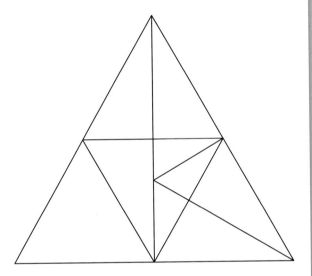

Sounds Like . . .

Find all the "oo" (as in "cool") and "i" (as in "bit") sounds that can be found in the text below:

> This was absolutely ridiculous! Gregory simply couldn't believe what his wife was putting him through. Wasn't it enough that he had to suffer sitting in that overcrowded drawing room, with all of those sick people coughing all over him, just to listen to some girl playing a flute? Now she expected him to listen to a bassoon player, too? Gregory was thoroughly disgusted with the whole situation and stormed out of the recital, stubbing his toe along the way, vowing never to return.

What's the point?

It is difficult to spot the right sounds as their graphic shape changes. For example, the "oo" sound can be written "o," "oo," "ou," or even "u." Likewise, all "i"s are not pronounced the same.

Sounds Like . . .

Find all the "a" (as in "say") and "i" (as in "ice") sounds that can be found in the text below:

Isis loved geography—she could stare at a globe for hours. She would imagine traveling to such far away places as Ireland, Asia, Malaysia, Indonesia, Iceland, and Hawaii. She would even book entire itineraries in her mind. The flights she'd take! The sights she'd see! On her imaginary trip to Italy, she would definitely stop in Pompeii, travel along the Appian Way, and then head to Pisa to see the leaning tower. She sighed. The wonders of India, of China, of Bahrain! She'd get there one day, she promised herself. One day.

Did you know?
Your focused attention is being given a workout in this exercise!

The Missing Tile

Which of the four tiles below completes the picture?

What's the point?

When working on a jigsaw puzzle, you can rely not only on the patterns, but also on the shape of the piece itself. In this exercise, however, all pieces have the same shape, they are only one color, and you can't even move the pieces to see if they will fit!

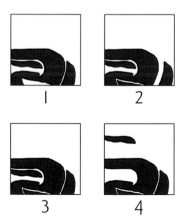

1   2

3   4

The Missing Tile

Which of the four tiles below completes the picture?

Did you know?
American researchers have recently shown that video games, especially action games, improve levels of visual attention, thus making it more efficient and reliable!

1

2

3

4

Word Search!

Find the fourteen words hidden in the grid. They can be read horizontally, vertically, or diagonally; backward or forward; up or down. The same letter can be used in several words.

HINT: the theme is **clothes**.

Tips

Try to find and apply a method to locate the words. It will make your search much easier. For instance, you might methodically proceed row by row, then column by column to find words.

```
S  D  E  A  V  N  E  J  K  T  K  L
F  M  T  M  S  D  S  G  U  I  H  K
V  N  R  R  U  E  E  H  J  T  H  G
E  W  I  C  O  T  T  O  N  V  G  N
T  G  K  H  W  V  S  E  B  S  Z  O
T  F  S  R  E  S  U  O  R  T  O  L
E  S  N  D  E  N  I  M  C  O  S  Y
P  Z  A  Z  D  F  T  D  A  C  S  N
E  A  F  J  L  Y  B  F  P  K  E  S
O  V  C  H  V  J  H  K  X  I  R  O
H  V  L  A  U  N  D  R  Y  N  D  E
S  C  D  T  N  E  M  R  A  G  N  G
```

Word Search!

Find the fifteen words hidden in the grid. They can be read horizontally, vertically, or diagonally; backward or forward; up or down. The same letter can be used in several words.

HINT: the theme is **family**.

What's the point?

Two different types of attention and memory are involved in this exercise. First there is semantic memory—the vocabulary you have all stockpiled over the years. This exercise also activates your working memory, which helps you remember what letters did not match so that you don't waste time making the same mistake again!

F	G	B	J	R	A	R	E	Y	U	K	V
A	F	S	F	R	Y	M	M	U	M	Y	I
Q	N	A	A	D	O	P	T	I	O	N	F
H	E	J	D	C	C	T	C	Z	B	Z	H
Z	R	N	N	K	I	N	S	H	I	P	E
F	D	S	O	R	I	E	H	H	R	A	R
D	L	S	E	S	Z	R	J	E	T	P	E
S	I	B	U	N	Z	A	J	Z	H	A	H
D	H	O	H	F	E	P	D	V	K	R	T
A	C	C	D	A	U	G	H	T	E	R	A
D	Y	T	S	A	N	Y	D	L	T	P	F
O	I	D	Y	G	O	L	A	E	N	E	G

Alphabetical Disorder

Take a careful look at these two sets of characters. Take one minute to find out which characters appear in the series on the right but not the series on the left.

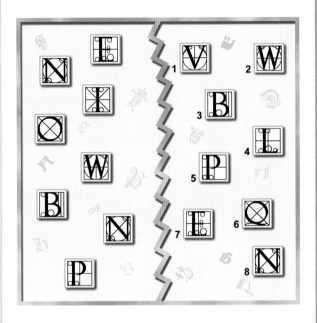

Take it to the next level

Memorize and then hide the series on the left. Which characters in the series on the right were not in the series on the left? By doing this, you'll add a memory component—specifically short-term memory with limited storage capacity—to this exercise.

Alphabetical Disorder

Take a careful look at these two sets of characters. Take one minute to find out which characters appear in the series on the right but not the series on the left.

Tips

Certain strategies, such as dividing a task into subtasks so that you have to focus for a shorter while on each subtask, might help you if you are having difficulties paying complete attention to these exercises.

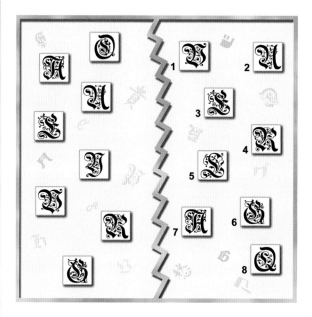

What's Wrong with this Picture?

Read the following story and pick out the four things that don't quite make sense.

This morning Jane had difficulty getting her young horse out of its stable. She tried to talk to him softly and persuade him to get out but nothing worked, and the beautiful Friesian would not budge. The caretaker was a bit worried because the race was to happen the next day, April 31, and the horse was showing signs of not wanting to run. It was necessary to train today, especially since tomorrow's race would probably be the last before its retirement from competition. When the horse finally decided to walk out on the leaf-covered ground, he looked sad and depressed, and Jane finally noticed that one of his legs looked sore and that he limped a bit. She called the vet immediately. He reassured her, telling her it was nothing serious.

What's the point?

Understanding text and figuring out what's wrong with it relies very much on memory and attention. Temporary memory stores a great amount of information and builds upon itself as we read in order for the text to make sense. However, your memory cannot store all the elements. In order to run efficiently, it only stores the most relevant elements (keywords and main ideas); irrelevant or repeated information is routinely removed from memory. Exercises like this help keep that kind of memory sharp and focused.

What's Wrong with this Picture?

Read the following story and pick out the four things that don't quite make sense.

After the six-hour flight from Dallas, Mary and Dave finally landed in Sydney for their three-week honeymoon, anxious to embark on the vacation of their dreams. After leaving the luggage at the hotel, the young Texan couple decided to take a tour on an open-top bus to get a first glimpse of the city. And they became enchanted by it. Hand in hand, they wandered carelessly for hours in the lively streets, without feeling any fatigue from the jet lag. After a few days more in Sydney, they ventured inland, where they met incredible people and even more incredible animals. Dave, a fan of reptiles, was completely awed by all the strange and wonderful creatures they encountered, while his fiancée was much more taken with the kangaroos, koalas, and pandas they saw. One week later, when they were showing their pictures to their friends back in Texas, they were astonished to learn that they had shot more than a thousand photographs! They gave the address of their travel agent to whomever wanted it, because they had such a wonderful time in the land down under.

Did you know?

We all have the capacity to focus on particulars while making an abstraction of the surroundings. However, a recent study has shown that anxious people find it more difficult to focus and are more likely to be disturbed by unessential details when engaging in an exercise like this.

The Odd One Out

Find the odd one out in each series.

✳✳✳✳✳✳✳✳✳✳✳✳✳✳✳✳✳✳✳✳✳✳✳✳
✳✳✳✳✳✳✳✳✳✳✳✳✳✳✳✳✳✳✳✳✳✳✳✳
✳✳✳✳✳✳✳✳✳✳✳✳✳✳✳✳✳✳✳✳✳✳✳✳
✳✳✳✳✳✳✳✳✳✳✳✳✳✳✳✳✳✳✳✳✳✳✳✳
✳✱✳✳✳✳✳✳✳✳✳✳✳✳✳✳✳✳✳✳✳✳✳✳

H H H H H H H H H H H H H H H H H H H H H H H H
H H H H H H H H H H H H H H H H H H H H H H H H
H H H H H H H H H H H H H H H H H H H H H H H H
H H H H H H H H Π H H H H H H H H H H H H H H H
H H H H H H H H H H H H H H H H H H H H H H H H

ᴐᴐᴐᴐᴐᴐᴐᴐᴐᴐᴐᴐᴐᴐᴐᴐᴐᴐᴐᴐᴐᴐᴐᴐᴐᴐᴐᴐᴐᴐᴐᴐᴐᴐᴐᴐᴐᴐ
ᴐᴐᴐᴐᴐᴐᴐᴐᴐᴐᴐᴐᴐᴐᴐᴐᴐᴐᴐᴐᴐᴐᴐᴐᴐᴐᴐᴐᴐᴐᴐᴐᴐᴐᴐᴐᴐᴐ
ᴐᴐᴐᴐᴐᴐᴐᴐᴐᴐᴐᴐᴐᴐᴐᴐᴐᴐᴐᴐᴐᴐᴐᴐᴐᴐᴐᴐᴐᴐᴐᴐᴐᴐᴅᴐᴐᴐ
ᴐᴐᴐᴐᴐᴐᴐᴐᴐᴐᴐᴐᴐᴐᴐᴐᴐᴐᴐᴐᴐᴐᴐᴐᴐᴐᴐᴐᴐᴐᴐᴐᴐᴐᴐᴐᴐᴐ
ᴐᴐᴐᴐᴐᴐᴐᴐᴐᴐᴐᴐᴐᴐᴐᴐᴐᴐᴐᴐᴐᴐᴐᴐᴐᴐᴐᴐᴐᴐᴐᴐᴐᴐᴐᴐᴐᴐ

Did you know?

When you drive, it is crucial that you stay focused and that your attention levels remain high. This is why many countries have made it illegal to make phone calls while driving and why train conductors have to check in regularly while on long journeys.

The Odd One Out

Find the odd one out in each series.

The Connecting Thread

Try to find the logical order of the pictures below.

Tips

Sometimes the order of the pictures is chronological; sometimes it is just logical. Once you've established this, you can then build up a story to link one picture to another. In more complex situations, you may have to guess that another event has taken place in between two pictures.

Seeing Is Believing

Study the picture carefully for two minutes. Then turn the page for the next step of the exercise.

Tips

This is a difficult exercise that requires a high level of visual attention. You might divide the pictures into zones (foreground, swimming pool, buildings, sky) to make memorization easier.

Seeing Is Believing

Answer the following questions.

1. How many people are there in the swimming pool?

_____

2. Is there someone on the diving board?

_____

3. What color is the swimming suit of the blonde woman in the foreground?

_____

4. Can you see the sun in the picture?

_____

5. What shape is the child's buoy in the swimming pool?

_____

6. How many different types of trees are there?

_____

Seeing Is Believing

Study the picture carefully for two minutes. Then turn the page for the next step of the exercise.

Did you know?

What we call "observation" is really the visual memory and attention you use every day. These processes enable you to notice that your neighbor has bought a new car, that your friend Jessica and your sister have the same dress, or that your colleague has redecorated her office.

Seeing Is Believing

Answer the following questions:

1. How many baguettes does the customer have under his arm?

   _____

2. What is the price shown on the register?

   _____

3. What color is the man's scarf?

   _____

4. How many croissants are there in the display cabinet?

   _____

5. How many spotlights are there on the ceiling?

   _____

6. Is the woman wearing a jacket?

   _____

Difficult Exercises

Pencils Up!

Link the twelve stars with sixteen points on this page without raising your pencil.

You cannot touch the other shapes, and you cannot go between two figures more than once!

Did you know?

The fact that the shapes are similar in shape and color makes this a more difficult exercise. This should stretch your visual attention to the limit!

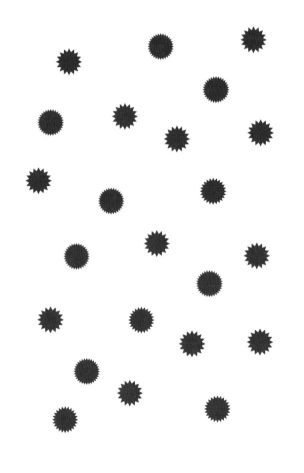

Pencils Up!

Link the twelve hexagons on this page without raising your pencil.

You cannot touch the other shapes, and you cannot go between two figures more than once!

Tips

If you find yourself having a hard time with this one, find a quiet, peaceful place to try again. Don't give up!

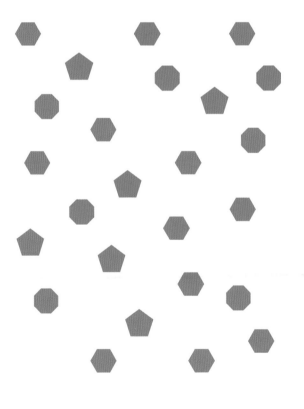

Pay Attention to Words

You have one minute to memorize the ten words below, without looking at the second half of the page.

ANT	LIGHTNESS
PAINT	FLOWER
EXIT	OUTLET
LIGHTNING	BEE
AUNT	LIGHTWEIGHT

Now hide the words and answer these five questions:

1. Name the two synonyms on the list.

   _____

2. Were any insect names listed? If so, what?

   _____

3. Three words started with the same word fragment. What were they?

   _____

4. Two words were identical except for one letter. What were they?

   _____

5. Were there any words with more than nine letters? If so, what were they?

   _____

What's the point?

This exercise works your semantic recognition capacities and your ability to analyze word properties like homonyms, synonyms, compounds, meanings, and so on.

Pay Attention to Words

You have one minute to memorize the ten words below, without looking at the second half of the page.

SEA	**CROISSANT**
COLD	**DEATH**
TEACHER	**BOOKSELLER**
SEE	**CROWD**
CASTING	**BURN**

Now hide the words and answer these five questions:

1. What French word appears on the list?

   _____

2. How many words began with "C"? What were they?

   _____

3. What occupations were on the list?

   _____

4. Were there any homonyms on the list? What were they?

   _____

5. How many words had four letters? What were they?

   _____

Take it to the next level

Try memorizing the ten words more deeply and writing them down the next day on a piece of paper. Doing this transfers the words to your long-term memory, which enables you to store a greater amount of information than short-term memory and without any time limitations.

It Takes Two

Which two waiters are exactly alike?

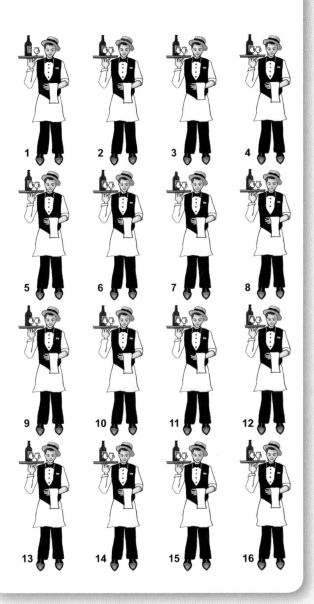

Did you know?

Like all brain functions, visual acuity can be trained and strengthened by regular and varied exercises like this!

It Takes Two

Which two rock stars are exactly alike?

Take it to the next level

Try this exercise the other way around. Memorize the numbers of the two pictures that are exactly similar, then the following day try to list all of the details that helped you figure out which ones didn't match up. This will add a memorization component to the initial exercise.

The Right Words

Read the text below, paying particular attention to nouns.

It was difficult to fathom how Johanna's parents—two respectable, middle-class people—had raised a child with such attitude! While the girl's mind was undoubtedly sharp as a tack, she was absolutely incorrigible. She had absolutely no regard for the feelings of others, she had the world's worst temper, her behavior was atrocious—all in all she was rotten to the core. Normally, Professor Bowman—like most teachers at the academy—was willing to bend the rules a bit if one of his pupils acted up, but not in Johanna's case. He had absolutely zero confidence that her tendency to act up could be corrected. She'd be expelled if he had anything to do with it. He would be glad to be rid of her.

Now hide the text and try and remember which nouns appeared in the story.

rules	teachers	mood
trend	pupils	confidence
child	mind	regulations
professor	character	tendency
kid	respect	behavior
aggressiveness	synergy	position
temper	attitude	

What's the point?

The exercise is much more difficult at this level for several reasons. The text is longer, so memorization is more complex and needs more attention. There are also more nouns both in the story itself and on the list of words to pick them from.

The Right Words

Read the text below, paying particular attention to nouns.

Megan wasn't able to sleep the evening before the Bluebell Derby. She always got nervous the day before a race—ever since the accident, her anxiety levels skyrocketed whenever she even thought about getting on her horse, let alone racing him in one of the biggest races of the year. She was terrified that he would jump on his hind legs out of fear like he did so many years ago, when he threw Megan from the saddle in the middle of the All States Equestrian Event. Ever since that horrible day, Megan's confidence problem had definitely become an issue. She hated to admit it, but she was no longer able to trust her horse the way she once did. This thought saddened her as she lay quietly in the dark, hoping for sleep to come.

Now hide the text and try and remember which nouns appeared in the story.

night	**trust**	**issue**
fright	**nothing**	**donkey**
day	**accident**	**problem**
incident	**track**	**fear**
lane	**flight**	**occurrence**
horse	**event**	

Take it to the next level

This exercise calls you to train your visual attention. If you want to give your auditory attention a workout, ask someone to read the text to you aloud, and then try to pick the nouns out from the list provided.

Easy as One-Two-Three

Take a careful look at the figure below and count the number of squares and triangles it has.

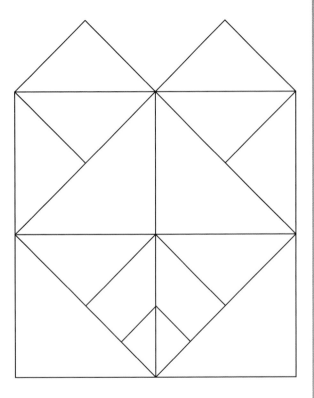

What's the point?

This exercise requires great spatial capacities, especially at this level of difficulty. Strong spatial abilities are crucial in helping you to evaluate distances, dimensions, and shapes of objects in daily life.

Easy as One-Two-Three

Take a careful look at the figure below and count the number of squares and triangles it has.

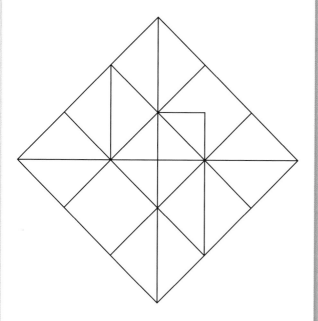

Did you know?

The recognition of shapes that enables you to spot squares and triangles contained in this figure is the same skill that enables you to recognize an object when it is partly hidden by something else.

Sounds Like . . .

Find all the "y" (as in "yell"), "w" (as in "wire"), and "ng" (as in "bring") sounds in the text below.

Sarah had to admit that this was going to be challenging. She stood at the edge of the pool watching her yellow slingback float in the water, trying to figure out how to retrieve it without getting wet. Standing on one foot staring at the mess her yard had become thanks to the ridiculous party Jan had thrown yesterday (she wouldn't waste any time getting her revenge on him, that was for sure), Sarah suddenly had an epiphany. She yanked a branch off the nearest tree, lay down on the diving board, and used the branch to slowly bring her precious footwear back to her, dodging the yellow rubber ducks someone had thrown in the pool sometime during the festivities.

Did you know?

The way a word looks can affect the reading speed. For instance, a word written alternatively with upper case and lower case letters will be less easy to recognize (RHytHm) and take you longer to read.

Sounds Like . . .

Find all the "th" (as in "path" and "the") and "s" (as in "sister") sounds in the text below.

There was nothing in the world that Timothy loved to do more than ice skate. It didn't matter if he skated alone or with friends; it didn't matter if he were in the fanciest rink in the world or on the small pond out back that sometimes froze in the middle of winter; it didn't matter what the weather was like outside; ice skating was Timothy's life. He had gotten quite skilled at it, too. He was able to do jumps and spins and salchows and toe loops and even a single axel without too many problems. As a result, he had been doing quite well in regional competitions—coming in fifth one year, fourth the next, and with any luck, he'd come in first this year. His coach seemed to think it was quite possible, and Timothy was going to go for it.

Did you know?

The consistency of a word within the context of the other words in a sentence is a large part of what makes reading possible. When you read a text, you intuitively expect what is going to follow, which speeds up the reading process. As a result, "she felt sorry for himself" does not "read" right, nor does "he got as green as a tomato."

The Missing Tile

There are two tiles missing in the figure below. Which two tiles complete the picture? Beware! Some tiles might have turned upside down!

What's the point?

At this difficult level, you can train your mental capacity for moving items at different angles. Some of the tiles need to be rotated in your mind to find out whether their patterns can be linked to the tile next to the blank square.

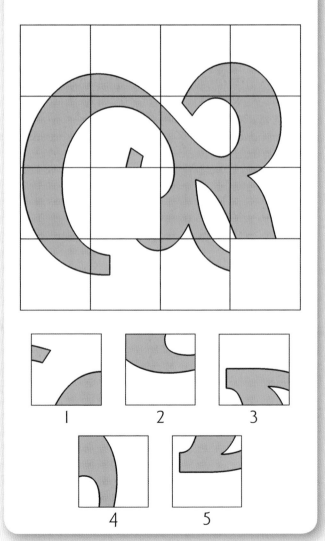

The Missing Tile

There are two tiles missing in the figure below. Which two tiles complete the picture? Beware! Some tiles might have turned upside down!

Did you know?

In daily life, mental rotation is used in all the activities of topographical orientation: reading a map, recognizing an object that is lying down when it should be standing up, and so on.

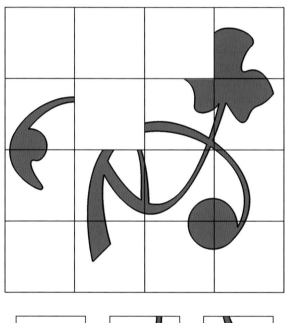

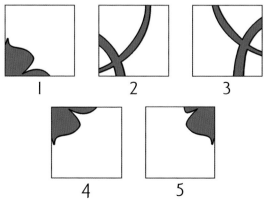

Word Search!

Find the twenty words hidden in the grid. They can be read horizontally, vertically, or diagonally; backward or forward; up or down. The same letter can be used in several words.

HINT: the theme is **animals**.

```
S D F G H T A F V A E C
W X R K R C H O O F E D
G H G H S E I C E P S F
H Z N Y I S F E K R D Y
T N I P A N T M U E Z G
O D L P E I O F X F J O
L D R U F N C A L F Z L
S B A P K V C B E A R O
B R E E D I N G P R C O
C F Y E N O X A K I O Z
W O L F I B W S S G V S
X V E L A M M A M D M E
```

What's the point?

This exercise, just like crosswords, improves your verbal flexibility—that is, the ability to find the relevant words exactly when you need them.

Word Search!

Find the twenty-one words hidden in the grid. They can be read horizontally, vertically, or diagonally; backward or forward; up or down. The same letter can be used in several words.

HINT: the theme is **plants and botanicals**.

```
T  R  E  E  G  A  R  D  E  N  N  M
A  F  C  Z  G  E  Z  P  A  R  K  O
J  T  R  V  J  T  D  O  G  E  I  S
F  R  E  V  R  G  E  R  L  F  D  S
N  U  E  N  I  E  E  C  A  X  U  W
E  N  W  W  B  P  S  E  K  G  J  N
H  K  T  I  O  N  L  U  N  V  F  R
C  T  D  L  K  L  D  U  N  G  D  W
I  F  L  L  A  O  F  H  E  D  E  B
L  E  E  O  O  H  B  C  E  Z  E  V
N  G  R  W  G  E  H  E  F  E  W  W
H  O  R  T  I  C  U  L  T  U  R  E
```

Did you know?

The type of focused attention required by this exercise is precisely the kind of attention that detectives and investigators call upon when they want to find evidence at a crime scene. They have no predefined idea of what they are looking for; they just let their attention be drawn by interesting items.

Alphabetical Disorder

Take a careful look at these two sets of characters. Take one minute to find out which characters appear in the series on the right but not the series on the left.

What's the point?

A strange noise or unusual event will draw your attention spontaneously whereas here willful attention is called upon, which requires a true cognitive effort. Indeed, you have to focus and draw your attention on a given target and process the information while you hear or see it.

Alphabetical Disorder

Take a careful look at these two sets of characters. Take one minute to find out which characters appear in the series on the right but not the series on the left.

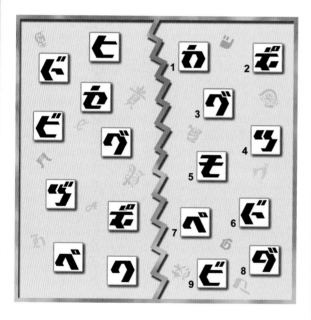

Did you know?

More and more human-resource managers ask potential employees to take tests in addition to the usual interview. They test logic, reasoning capacities, comprehension, and memory but also levels of attention. To excel at these tests, you will certainly find it useful to train with exercises such as this one. Scientific studies have shown that all of these functions can be improved thanks to training.

What's Wrong with this Picture?

Read the following story and pick out the five things that don't quite make sense.

Brian dreamed of becoming a doctor and, if possible, to become part of a humanitarian organization that brought medical assistance to the poor all around the world. He had vacationed in Bamako, Senegal, for a week in between his freshman and junior years of college and immediately fell in love with that part of the world and felt a calling to help the poor in that region. After that eye-opening experience, he took part in the organization of an AIDS vaccination campaign in West Africa and wanted to stay behind after his tour of duty was over. He had also met several "doctors with a mission" over the years, and as they told him incredible tales about all of the countries they visited, he couldn't wait to be done with the three years of medical school to get out in the world and do some good. While his beloved girlfriend, Nelly, found his motives admirable, she certainly didn't want to live in West Africa! She did not like animals for a start, and the idea of waking up in the morning to find that a puma had invaded their bedroom during the night was less than thrilling!

What's the point?

This exercise calls upon your semantic memory, as the incongruities in the story are partly cultural; this exercise calls upon your general knowledge of history, culture, geography, and art, among other things.

Therefore, to spot the out-of-place elements you will need not only to call upon your comprehension and analytical abilities, but also on your knowledge of facts.

What's Wrong with this Picture?

Read the following story and pick out the five things that don't quite make sense.

New York's greatest park, built in the 1920s, was a perfect place for lovebirds to meet up for a cozy lunch or a romantic dinner under the stars. There was nothing Lee loved more than meeting Simon for a quick bite to eat. Coming to Central Park was her escape from her overbearing mother, the nosy neighbors, and the overprotective teachers at her high school. An orphan since she was four, she couldn't wait to have her own family, to have many children, to recreate the family life that had been denied her. And she wanted to create this family with her beloved Simon. Though he was only seventeen, he was so much older than she was, so much more worldly and sophisticated. She was secretly hoping that he'd propose before being shipped off to the war next week. She allowed herself to dream of their wedding, imagining her father walking her down the aisle, Simon slipping a ring on her finger, celebrating afterward with her family and friends. She sat there looking up at the beautiful green leaves of Central Park as the snow fell heavily around her, waiting for her love to come.

Did you know?

Any text comprehension task relies on three preliminary types of knowledge:

- general knowledge of the world
- knowledge of language
- knowledge of the goal to be reached

In this exercise, for instance, the reader knows she must look out for strange elements; therefore, she will process the information carefully to find them.

The Odd One Out

In each series, find the given symbol.

The symbol to find is: ⊙

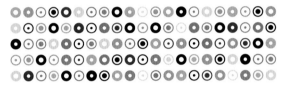

The symbol to find is: ✐

The symbol to find is: ✳

Did you know?
Many teenagers find it difficult to focus. This may be due to lack of sleep, lack of motivation, raging hormones, or lack of self-esteem. In order to improve their attention abilities, it might be helpful to have them think about their attention challenges objectively.

The Odd One Out

In each series, find the given symbol.

The symbol to find is: 🕐

The symbol to find is: ☁

The symbol to find is: ◈

Take it to the next level

This exercise obviously focuses on training visual attention. To train your auditory attention, you can listen to a song and then ask someone who can read the lyrics to ask you questions about it ("Did it contain the word 'happiness?'," "How many times was the chorus sung?").

The Connecting Thread

Try to find the logical order of the pictures below

Did you know?

In order to test the planning and strategy capacities of its astronauts, NASA makes them take a battery of tests. For instance, for one test, they have to make a list of objects, from the least important one to the most important, according to various critical situations they might find themselves facing. For example: You make a catastrophic landing in a country devastated by civil war. You have to abandon the plane. What do you take with you first?

- a bottle of water
- a gun
- a distress rocket
- a life jacket

Seeing Is Believing

Study the picture carefully for two minutes. Then turn the page for the next step of the exercise.

Did you know?

Currently, some researchers are working on the creation of visual attention sensors. These sensors would be able to detect whether the attention of, for example, the user of a mobile phone or computer is already at work or whether his attention levels are idle and can handle another task!

Seeing Is Believing

Answer the following questions:

1. How many kids are playing jump rope?

_____

2. What is the boy in the foreground eating, an apple or a banana?

_____

3. What time is it in the picture?

_____

4. Are there clouds in the sky?

_____

5. On which square of the hopscotch is the little girl standing?

_____

6. How many basketball baskets are there in the yard?

_____

7. What color hat is the girl who is playing marbles wearing?

_____

8. Is the teacher holding the briefcase in her right or left hand?

_____

Seeing Is Believing

Study the picture carefully for two minutes. Then turn the page for the next step of the exercise.

Take it to the next level

Take a look at the picture for two minutes and ask someone else to come up with new questions for you to answer.

To make it even more difficult, you can try to recreate the picture yourself by drawing it from memory on a separate sheet of paper, with as many details as possible. You might well be surprised by the result!

Seeing Is Believing

Answer the following questions:

1. What is the name of the garage?

   _____

2. Are there bars on the windows?

   _____

3. How many tires are piled next to the garage door?

   _____

4. Is the license plate of the blue car visible?

   _____

5. What color is the car on the lift?

   _____

6. Is there a screwdriver showing out of the mechanic's pocket?

   _____

7. How many beams can you see on the roof?

   _____

8. What does the can on the left bottom side of the picture contain?

   _____

Solutions

Easy Exercises

Pay Attention to Words (page 4)
1. There are three adjectives: soft, rude, greedy.
2. There are two animal names: turtle, deer.
3. There is one abstract concept: happiness.

Pay Attention to Words (page 5)
1. Three words start with "F": friend, fright, folly.
2. There is one tree name: pine.
3. The longest word in the list is: alphabet.

It Takes Two (page 6)
The two perfectly identical characters are #3 and #7. The details that eliminate the other possibilities are:

    #1: the tip of the umbrella is not visible

    #2: a pattern is missing from the back of the geisha's belt

    #4: the geisha's back foot is more obscured by her kimono

    #5: the stem of the umbrella is more visible

    #6: the ribbon in the geisha's hair is a different color

    #8: the geisha's left eyebrow is missing

    #9: a floral pattern is missing on the kimono

It Takes Two (page 7)
The two perfectly identical birds are #2 and #9. The details that eliminate the other possibilities are:

    #1: there is less black above the stork's right leg

    #3: the bottom part of the beak is in front of the bundle

    #4: a joint is missing on the stork's right leg

    #5: the gray part is less big

    #6: a straw strand is missing from the nest's left side

    #7: a gray part is missing under the white part

    #8: the black end of the stork's wing is missing

The Right Words (page 8)
The adjectives in the text are: dangerous, local, true, strangest, long.

The Right Words (page 9)
The adjectives in the text are: distinct, medieval, great, frequent, modern.

Easy as One-Two-Three (page 10)
There are 20 squares in this figure (11 small ones, 7 medium ones, 1 big one, and 1 overarching one).

Easy as One-Two-Three (page 11)
There are 9 squares in this figure (5 small ones, 3 medium ones, 1 overarching one).

Sounds Like . . . (page 12)
The "sh" sounds are in italics in the text below.

*Sh*e was so well-liked and respected in the neighborhood that no one suspected that *sh*e had been cheating on her husband for years! *Sh*e aroused absolutely no sus*pi*cions. *Sh*e went to church week after week and confessed the most hideous sins to the pari*sh* priest without any sense of *sh*ame or remorse. Her friends were quite *s*ure *sh*e was honest and good natured and had no idea how depraved *sh*e really was!

Sounds Like . . . (page 13)
The "f" sounds are in italics in the text below.

As *Ph*ilip drank his co*ff*ee, he silently prayed *f*or things to go smoothly. Tracking Sarah down in the jungles of the *Ph*ilippines was just the *f*irst *ph*ase of the plan. Getting her on the plane and bringing her home was going to be the tricky part—*Ph*ilip would be *f*oolish to think otherwise. If Sarah didn't *f*eel sa*f*e back in Akron, she would certainly *f*lee once again. *F*or this plan to work out to the satis*f*action of everyone involved, he would have to be exceedingly care*f*ul.

The Missing Tile (page 14)
The missing tile is #1.

The Missing Tile (page 15)

The missing tile is #3.

Word Search! (page 16)

The hidden words are: VIOLIN, SONATA, CELLO, MELODY, SYMPHONY, BLUEGRASS, RHYTHM, PULSE, BAND, INTERPRET

They are in red in the grid below.

Word Search! (page 17)

The hidden words are: MAIZE, VEGETABLES, TOMATO, OIL, LIME, BREAD, TUNA, ONION, PASTA, PIZZA

They are in red in the grid below.

```
G  H  F  Y  G  B  U  I  L  V  N  Z
G  S  F  Q  H  K  S  A  D  F  E  Y
C  V  E  K  N  R  F  X  D  R  B  K
A  V  V  L  E  F  A  D  B  G  C  N
D  A  E  R  B  O  N  I  O  N  Z  S
H  A  G  V  B  A  U  C  X  W  B  S
Q  T  G  B  Z  J  T  S  N  L  M  Y
C  S  I  Z  S  H  O  E  J  I  K  C
D  A  I  S  N  H  M  Z  G  M  R  H
X  P  F  G  H  M  A  I  Z  E  C  B
Z  V  H  Y  J  K  T  D  B  E  V  S
Z  B  A  D  L  I  O  D  F  B  E  Z
```

Alphabetical Disorder (page 18)

The characters that can be found only on the right are #2, #3, and #7.

Alphabetical Disorder (page 19)

The characters that can be found only on the right are #4 and #6.

What's Wrong with this Picture? (page 20)

The three strange elements are:

- Ms. Cole couldn't have driven her son to school if her car was packed from passenger's seat to the trunk.
- She couldn't have looked into her rearview mirror for the same reason.
- She couldn't have driven her son to school on Christmas Day.

What's Wrong with this Picture? (page 21)
The three weird elements are:
- Caroline was hired in August, so there would have been no need to find a shelter against the cold.
- The building has five floors, so the fourth one cannot be the top.
- No book can be more than seven centuries old because printing had not been invented at that point in history.

The Odd One Out (page 22)
The odd one out is number 5, line 3.
The odd one out is number 2, line 1.
The odd one out is number 15, line 2.

The Odd One Out (page 23)
The odd one out is number 2 from right to left, line 4.
The odd one out is number 4, line 2.
The odd one out is number 9 from right to left, line 3.

The Connecting Thread (page 24)
The correct order is #3, #6, #1, #2, #4, #5.

Seeing Is Believing (page 25)
1. The vendor holds a bottle in his left hand.
2. The horse that is leading the race wears number 2.
3. The woman with a purple suit is wearing a hat.
4. There are five horses in the picture.

Seeing Is Believing (page 27)
1. The vase is blue.
2. The painting on the wall shows a fishing boat on a beach.
3. The window is shut.
4. There are no books near the TV.

Medium Exercises

Pay Attention to Words (page 32)
1. The adverb is: roughly.
2. The two shortest words are: bed, tea.
3. There are three pieces of furniture listed: bed, stool, sofa.
4. The flower name is: orchid.

Pay Attention to Words (page 33)
1. Two words end with "erry": cranberry, ferry.
2. The plural word is: children.
3. Two words have five letters: piano, ferry.
4. The word associated with fish is: net.

It Takes Two (page 34)
The two perfectly identical characters are #4 and #7. The details that eliminate the other possibilities are:
> #1: a tuft of hair is missing on the dragon's head
> #2: a black line is missing under its left ear
> #3: the black line on its neck is shorter
> #5: the first spine of its crest is missing
> #6: the black line of its jaw is shorter
> #8: a spine is missing on the right wing
> #9: a tooth is missing
> #10: a claw is missing on the right paw
> #11: the end of the tail is different
> #12: the black line on the thigh is smaller

It Takes Two (page 35)
The two perfectly identical characters are #9 and #10. The details that eliminate the other possibilities are:
> #1: a stripe is missing on the right sleeve of the policeman
> #2: a black line is missing on his left boot
> #3: the gun's case is missing
> #4: his left hand's thumb is missing

#5: a button is missing on his jacket
#6: one side of his jacket is shorter
#7: the badge is missing on his hat
#8: the red border is missing on the left sleeve
#11: the shield on the jacket is different
#12: a crease is missing on the left sleeve elbow

The Right Words (page 36)
The verbs in the text are: realized, traveled, experienced, packed, found, went, persuaded, convinced, abandoned

The Right Words (page 37)
The verbs in the text are: stood up, walked, watched, entertained, enjoyed, play, appreciate

Easy as One-Two-Three (page 38)
There are twenty triangles in this figure.

Easy as One-Two-Three (page 39)
There are twenty-three triangles in this figure.

Sounds Like . . . (page 40)
The "oo" and "i" sounds are in italics in the text below.
   Th*i*s was absol*u*tely r*i*d*i*culous! Gregory s*i*mply couldn't believe what h*i*s wife was putting h*i*m thr*oo*gh. Wasn't *i*t enough that he had to suffer s*i*tting *i*n that overcrowded drawing r*oo*m, with all of those s*i*ck people coughing all over h*i*m, just to l*i*sten to some girl playing a flute? Now she expected h*i*m to l*i*sten to a bass*oo*n player, t*oo*? Gregory was thoroughly d*i*sgusted with the whole s*i*tuation and stormed out of the recital, stubbing h*i*s toe along the way, vowing never to return.

Sounds Like . . . (page 41)
The "a" and "i" sounds are in italics in the text below.
   *I*sis loved geography—she could st*a*re at a globe for hours. She would imagine traveling to such far *a*w*a*y pl*a*ces as *I*reland, *A*sia, Mal*a*ysia, Indonesia, *I*celand, and Hawaii. She would even book ent*i*re *i*tineraries

in her mind. The flights she'd take! The sights she'd see! On her imaginary trip to Italy, she would definitely stop in Pompeii, travel along the Appian Way, and then head to Pisa to see the leaning tower. She sighed. The wonders of India, of China, of Bahrain! She'd get there one day, she promised herself. One day.

The Missing Tile (page 42)
The missing tile is #3.

The Missing Tile (page 43)
The missing tile is #4.

Word Search! (page 44)
The hidden words are: TROUSERS, STOCKING, GARMENT, COSTUME, DRESS, SUIT, DENIM, COTTON, SKIRT, NYLON, SHOE, HAT, CAP, LAUNDRY
They are in red in the grid below.

S	D	E	A	V	N	E	J	K	T	K	L
F	M	T	M	S	D	S	G	U	I	H	K
V	N	R	R	U	E	E	H	J	T	H	G
E	W	I	C	O	T	T	O	N	V	G	N
T	G	K	H	W	V	S	E	B	S	Z	O
T	F	S	R	E	S	U	O	R	T	O	L
E	S	N	D	E	N	I	M	C	O	S	Y
P	Z	A	Z	D	F	T	D	A	C	S	N
E	A	F	J	L	Y	B	F	P	K	E	S
O	V	C	H	V	J	H	K	X	I	R	X
H	V	L	A	U	N	D	R	Y	N	D	E
S	C	D	T	N	E	M	R	A	G	N	G

Word Search! (page 45)

The hidden words are: PARENT, COUSIN, CHILDREN, GENEALOGY, SON, DAUGHTER, KINSHIP, HEIR, FATHER, PAPA, MUMMY, DYNASTY, BIRTH, GENES, ADOPTION

They are in red in the grid below.

Alphabetical Disorder (page 46)

The characters that can be found only on the right are #1, #4, and #6.

Alphabetical Disorder (page 47)

The characters that can be found only on the right are #5 and #8.

What's Wrong with this Picture? (page 48)

The four strange elements are:

- A Friesian is not a race horse; it's a show horse.
- If the horse is young, there is no reason for him to "retire" from competition.
- There are only thirty days in April.
- There are no dead leaves in April.

What's Wrong with this Picture? (page 49)

The four strange elements are:

- Flights from Texas to Sydney take more than six hours.
- The couple is on honeymoon, so Mary is not Dave's fiancée, she is his wife.
- Pandas are not native to Australia.
- The honeymoon is said to last three weeks, but they are showing photographs to their friends less than a week later.

The Odd One Out (page 50)

The odd one out is number 2, line 5.
The odd one out is number 9, line 4.
The odd one out is number 5 from right to left, line 3.

The Odd One Out (page 51)

The odd one out is number 10, line 3.
The odd one out is number 1, line 5.
The odd one out is number 2, line 4.

The Connecting Thread (page 52)

The correct order is #6, #3, #8, #2, #5, #1, #4, #7.

Seeing Is Believing (page 53)

1. There are four people in the pool.
2. There is nobody on the diving board.
3. The blonde woman is wearing a purple swimsuit.
4. The sun does appear in the picture.
5. The child's buoy is duck-shaped.
6. Two different types of trees can be seen in the picture.

Seeing Is Believing (page 55)

1. The customer holds two baguettes under his arm.
2. The price shown is $1.20.
3. The man's scarf is red.
4. There are five croissants in the display cabinet.
5. There are four spotlights on the ceiling.
6. The woman is not wearing a jacket.

Difficult Exercises

Pay Attention to Words (page 60)

1. The two synonyms are: exit, outlet.
2. The two insect names are: ant, bee.
3. The three words with the same prefix are: lightning, lightness, lightweight.
4. The two words that are only one letter different are: ant, aunt.
5. There is one word with more than nine letters: lightweight.

Pay Attention to Words (page 61)

1. The French word is: croissant.
2. Four words begin with a "C": cold, casting, croissant, crowd.
3. The two occupation names are: teacher, bookseller.
4. The two homonyms are: see, sea.
5. There are two words with four letters: cold, burn.

It Takes Two (page 62)

The two perfectly identical characters are #6 and #15. The details that eliminate the other possibilities are:

> #1: a glass is missing on the tray
> #2: the ribbon on the hat is of a different color
> #3: the napkin is shorter
> #4: the laces are missing on the left shoe
> #5: the badge is missing from the vest
> #7: the cork of the bottle is missing
> #8: a button is missing on the shirt
> #9: the bottle's label is missing
> #10: the seam is missing on the right sleeve of the shirt
> #11: the left hand's thumb is missing
> #12: the tray is smaller
> #13: the seam is missing on the left sleeve of the shirt
> #14: one finger of the right hand is shorter
> #16: the corner of the apron is less pointed

It Takes Two (page 63)

The two perfectly identical characters are #4 and #9. The details that eliminate the other possibilities are:

    #1: the pendant is missing from the man's neck chain

    #2: a tuft of hair is missing

    #3: a black button is missing on the guitar

    #5: a black line is missing on his left shoe

    #6: the pattern on his T-shirt is missing

    #7: the tattoo is missing on his right arm

    #8: the bracelet is missing on his right arm

    #10: a peg is missing on the guitar's neck

    #11: a crease in the pants is missing at left ankle's level

    #12: the black part of the guitar is smaller

    #13: the white part of the guitar is smaller

    #14: the bottom of the T-shirt is straight

    #15: the tuft of hair on the top of his head is shorter

    #16: his mouth is missing

The Right Words (page 64)

The nouns in the text are: rules, pupils, behavior, temper, teachers, confidence, mind, tendency, attitude, child.

The Right Words (page 65)

The nouns in the text are: issue, day, problem, fear, horse, accident, event.

Easy as One-Two-Three (page 66)

There are ten squares and twenty-four triangles in this figure.

Easy as One-Two-Three (page 67)

There are fifteen squares and thirty-seven triangles in this figure.

Sounds Like . . . (page 68)

The "y," "w," and "ng" sounds are in italics in the text below.

Sarah had to admit that this *w*as going to be challengi*ng*. She stood at edge of the pool *w*atchi*ng* her *y*ellow sli*ng*back float in the *w*ater, tryi*ng* to figure out ho*w* to retrieve it *w*ithout getti*ng* *w*et. Standi*ng* on one foot stari*ng* at the mess her *y*ard had become thanks to the ridiculous party Jan had thro*w*n *y*esterday (she *w*ouldn't *w*aste any time getti*ng* her revenge on him, that *w*as for sure), Sarah suddenly had an epiphany. She *y*anked a branch off the nearest tree, lay do*w*n on the divi*ng* board, and used the branch to slo*w*ly bri*ng* her precious foot*w*ear back to her, dodgi*ng* the *y*ellow rubber ducks someone had thro*w*n in the pool sometime duri*ng* the festivities.

Sounds Like . . . (page 69)

The "th" and "s" sounds are in italics in the text below.

*Th*ere was no*th*ing in the world *th*at Timo*th*y loved to do more *th*an ice *s*kate. It didn't matter if he *s*kated alone or wi*th* friends; it didn't matter if he were in the fancie*s*t rink in the world or on *th*e *s*mall pond out back *th*at *s*ometimes froze in the middle of winter; it didn't matter what *th*e wea*th*er was like out*s*ide; ice *s*kating was Timo*th*y'*s* life. He had gotten quite *s*killed at it, too. He was able to do jump*s* and *s*pins and *s*alchows and toe loop*s* and even a *s*ingle axel wi*th*out too many problem*s*. As a result, he had been doing quite well in regional competition*s*—coming in fif*th* one year, four*th* the next, and wi*th* any luck, he'd come in first *th*is year. His coach *s*eemed to *th*ink it was quite po*ss*ible, and Timo*th*y was going to go for it.

The Missing Tile (page 70)

The missing tiles are #3 and #4.

The Missing Tile (page 71)

The missing tiles are #1 and #2.

Word Search! (page 72)

The hidden words are: RHINO, MONKEY, GIRAFFE, CALF, YEARLING, BREEDING, BEE, INSECT, BEAR, PUPPY, ANT, LION, SPECIES, MAMMAL, FUR, SLOTH, HOOF, PAW, WOLF, ZOOLOGY.

They are in red in the grid below.

```
S  D  F  G  H  T  A  F  V  A  E  C
W  X  R  K  R  C  H  O  O  F  E  D
G  H  G  H  S  E  I  C  E  P  S  F
H  Z  N  Y  I  S  F  E  K  R  D  Y
T  N  I  P  A  N  T  M  U  E  Z  G
O  D  L  P  E  I  O  F  X  F  J  O
L  D  R  U  F  N  C  A  L  F  Z  L
S  B  A  P  K  V  C  B  E  A  R  O
B  R  E  E  D  I  N  G  P  R  C  O
C  F  Y  E  N  O  X  A  K  I  O  Z
W  O  L  F  I  B  W  S  S  G  V  S
X  V  E  L  A  M  M  A  M  D  M  E
```

Word Search! (page 73)

The hidden words are: TREE, GARDEN, LEAF, FUNGUS, MOSS, FLOWER, ALGAE, FERN, WILLOW, SEED, POLLEN, CROP, WOOD, OAK, HORTICULTURE, SUN, DEW, WEED, LICHEN, TWIG, TRUNK.

They are in red in the grid below.

Alphabetical Disorder (page 74)

The character that can be found only on the right is #5.

Alphabetical Disorder (page 75)

The characters that can be found only on the right are #1, #4, #5, and #8.

What's Wrong with this Picture? (page 76)

The five strange elements are:

- Bamako is not in Senegal; it is the capital city of Mali.
- The week's vacation should be between his freshman and sophomore years or sophomore and junior years.
- There is no vaccine against AIDS.
- It takes more than three years of study to be a doctor.
- There are no pumas in Africa, only in South America.

What's Wrong with this Picture? (page 77)

The five strange elements are:
- New York's Central Park was built in the 1860s, not 1920s.
- If Lee is an orphan, she does not have a mother.
- If Lee is an orphan, she does not have a father to walk her down the aisle.
- If Simon is only seventeen, he is too young to be shipped off to war.
- If it snows, the leaves cannot be green.

The Odd One Out (page 78)

The odd one out is number 1, line 4.
The odd one out is number 4 from right to left, line 5.
The odd one out is number 13, line 3.

The Odd One Out (page 79)

The odd one out is number 2 from right to left, line 2.
The odd one out is number 2, line 4.
The odd one out is number 9, line 5.

The Connecting Thread (page 80)

The correct order is #1, #6, #4, #8, #10, #9, #7, #3, #5, #2.

Seeing Is Believing (page 81)

1. Two kids are playing jump rope.
2. The boy in the foreground is eating an apple.
3. The clock does not show any time.
4. There are no clouds in the sky.
5. The little girl stands on the fifth square of the hopscotch.
6. There is one basketball basket in the yard.
7. The girl playing marbles is wearing a pink cap.
8. The teacher is not holding the briefcase in either hand.

Seeing Is Believing (page 83)

1. The name of the garage is Saroule.
2. There are no bars on the windows.
3. Five tires are piled next to the garage door.
4. The plate of the blue car cannot be seen.
5. The color of the car on the lift is red.
6. No screwdriver is showing out of the mechanic's pocket.
7. Two beams can be seen on the roof.
8. The can on the bottom left side of the picture contains oil.

References

Azouvi, P., Couillet, J., & Agar, N. (1998). Troubles de l'attention après traumatisme crânien sévère: Aspects théoriques et rééducation. *Revue de neuropsychologie,* 8(1), 125-154.

Baddeley, A.D. (1986). *Working memory.* New York: Oxford University Press.

Boujon, C., & Quaireau, C. (1997). *Attention et réussite scolaire.* Dunod.

Camus, J.-F. (1996). *La psychologie cognitive de l'attention.* Armand Colin/Masson.

Camus, J.-F. (1998). Neuropsychologie de l'attention: L'apport des réseaux attentionnels neurocérébraux. *Revue de neuropsychologie,* 8(1), 25-52.

Camus, J.-F., Gély-Nargeot, M.-C., & Michel, B.F. (2000). *Attention à la mémoire: Contribution et diagnostic précoce de la maladie d'Alzheimer.* Editions Solal.

Couillet, J., Leclercq, M., Moroni, C., & Azouvi, P. (Eds.) (2001). *La neuropsychologie de l'attention.* Marseille: Solal.

Falardeau, G. (1997). *Les enfants hyperactifs et lunatiques.* Editions du Jour.

Gazzaniga, M.S., Ivry, R., & Mangun, G.R. (2002). *Cognitive neuroscience: The biology of the mind.* DeBoeck Universite.

Honorez, J.-M. (2002). *Hyperactivité avec ou sans déficit d'attention. Un point de vue de l'épidémiologie scolaire.* Logiques Editions.

Jacques, T. (2001). *Trouble de l'attention impulsivité & hyperactivité chez l'enfant* (2nde édition). Editions Masson.

LaBerge, D. (1998). L'attention comme intensification de l'activité corticale. *Revue de neuropsychologie,* 8(1), 53-82.

Leclercq, M., & Zimmerman, P. (Eds.) (2002). *Applied neuropsychology of attention: Theory, diagnosis and rehabilitation.* Londres: Psychology Press.

Leclercq, M., Couillet, J., Azouvi, P., Marlier, N., Martin, Y., Strypstein, E., & Rousseaux, M. (2000). Dual task performance after severe diffuse traumatic brain injury or vascular prefrontal damage. *Journal of Clinical and Experimental Neuropsychology,* 22(3), 339-350.

Mateer, C.A., & Mapou, R. (1996). Understanding, evaluating and managing attention disorders following traumatic brain injury. *Journal of Head Trauma Rehabilitation*, 11(2), 1-16.

Mialer, J.-P. (1999). *L'attention*. Que Sais-Je numéro 3488, PUF.

Posner, M.I. (1980). Orienting of attention. *Quarterly Journal of Experimental Psychology*, 32, 3-25.

Richard, J.-F. (2000). *L'attention*. Presses Universitaires de France.

Seron, X., & Jeannerod, M. (1994). *Neuropsychologie humaine*. Liège: Mardaga.

Siéroff, E. (1998). Théories et paradigmes expérimentaux de l'attention. *Revue de neuropsychologie*, 8(1), 3-24.

Von Hofe, M. (1997). *Attention et contrôle cognitif. Mécanismes, développement des habiletés, pathologies*. Presses Universitaires de Rouen.

To get your mind in even sharper shape, visit:

www.happyneuron.com